Vertebrae

'Glyn Edwards' beautiful finely-wrought poems balance science and feeling, the stars and nature in a collection that adds up to the striking and intense life of one intelligent being. A brimming universality conveys a strange, familiar and exhilarating world.'

Martina Evans

'Glyn Edwards is a true original who is not swamped or drowned out by channelling his predecessors from Shakespeare and Dorothy Wordsworth to Dylan Thomas, Wilfred Owen, Ted Hughes and beyond. He brings his own sharp observation, deep feeling and gift for language to the mix and makes everything his own.

The bedrock of this collection is a tenderness grounded in love and empathy, starting with close family, but moving seamlessly out to bring that emotional openness to the contemplation of a drowned boy, an eccentric solitary, a lamb given a poignant monologue Les Murray would have been proud of, and historical figures such as the soldier poets of the first world war. Inanimate objects like boats and houses and outgrown baby clothes take on a life of their own. The poems of the natural world are breathtakingly vivid and the reader becomes gifted with the poet's ability to see with exceptional clarity and steadiness. And not just see, but feel for and about. These poems will sharpen your perceptions, refresh your thinking, and open your heart. What more could you want? Welcome a new bright star in poetry. 'I huddle into my coats / and hurry across the shore like a sandpiper.''

John Freeman

'Those of us who have watched the work of Glyn Edwards developing over a number of years know him to be an exciting and genuine poet, with a distinctive, elegant lyric voice. It is brilliant to see him delivering on this promise in a powerful, moving first collection. This is a poetry of the natural world and of memorable last lines, of *Wuthering Heights* and Moortown, of a half-built snowman which a speaker takes it upon himself to finish building for a neighbour. The poet writes particularly movingly about family and fatherhood, about a picture of his wife on his phone, or the process of sorting a baby's clothes once the child has outgrown them. Tender and varied, in touch with the darkness, these are poems to proclaim and sing, to celebrate and cherish.'

Jonathan Edwards

'Powerful and resonant. [Edwards] wants to connect with not confuse the reader. Deeply visceral, taking us into a world we sometimes only visit online in pieces such as 'Lambing Language.' …'Voicemail' moved me to tears…. A poet who knows where he is heading and unapologetically takes us there… into the landscape of rural Wales and his own searching, becoming mindscape. A fulfilling, moving and energising collection of poems crafted from the erudite heart. So refreshing to read.'

Patrick Jones

Vertebrae

poems by

Glyn Edwards

published by
THE LONELY PRESS

First published in 2019 by The Lonely Press Limited
62 Kings Road, Pontcanna, Cardiff, CF11 9DD, Wales

ISBN 978-1-9164987-5-4

Designed and typeset by John Lavin

Printed in Wales

Find out more about The Lonely Press and our literary journal, The Lonely Crowd at www.thelonelycrowd.org

For Nic and Arthur, always

Contents

Vertebrae

The Land or Body tide

The land or body tide, say the subtitles
    on the tv in the muted waiting room
            is the seismic force within the Earth
  diurnally displacing the solid surface
          in subtle peaks and depressions
    the camera lurches to long shot
            - the presenter lost in a vast quarry
  the curvature of sunset behind her -
          as imperceptible as the world turning
I notice your hand is trembling in mine
        the other quakes upon your stomach
but your stare is steadied at the screen
          - scientists cradling GPS equipment
  in unforgiving equatorial sunshine -
        tesseral movements up to half a metre
  prove gravity causes the rigid planet
        to contract in waves as it does water
  the obstetrician motions us so silently
        we follow to the ultrasound where you lie
I felt him surge last morning then stop
      you raise your dress lower your knickers
her camera orbits your taciturn womb
      exhuming nothing but a stilled chamber
excavating only subterranean gloom
      until the cardiograph leaps loud pulses
  a backbone intones on the monitor
      as pronounced as seams of strata
his body is bracing itself to absorb shock
      she plots the thirty-three spinal vertebrae
they're heavy enough to carry his mass
      the atlas bone is where his skull rests
  and the axis will allow his world to spin.
      Worlds form to endure pressure.

Night fishing

For decades my dreams were pike,
winched up from the barnacle dark,
febrile in the ugly dawn
and shameful of scrutiny.

At the spinning glint of a pen
or the lure of a bedside light
a pike would flex in my neck
as ruthless as a fired shell

and rise at the tense skin of sleep
and break it like glass. To trap it,
I'd force tired fingers down my throat
and catch the dense greengold gills

as they thrashed to be swallowed back
into a crypt of gut, then haul
it from my head in waking gloom
and wrap its snarl in puddled paper.

In the morning, on the yawning dresser,
I would weigh its mean physiognomy,
unbutton my flesh from its teeth
and find fluency in its jewelled flanks.

Later, I would relent my grip on its tail
and watch the denuded pike
descend in the printed page
until its candle eyes went dark.

I dream of carp now: basking
just below the milky surface,
anodyne and abbey pool bland,
floating shadows, too fat to land.

A Frontal Lobe Love Poem

Immediately after the battery has died
And the phone screen has turned black,
Sometimes, only sometimes,
Your face appears quickly on the glass.

And I don't tell you this, and I don't know quite why.
But the memory pulses when you say,
People's lives don't flash before them when they die,
You know? It's just electrical activity.

And I nod and pretend to read.
A neuroscientist from an American university
Studied rats that were clinically dead
And recorded their brain activity

With EEG electrodes. At cardiac arrest
When their match-head hearts were stilled
There's evidence of thirty seconds, no less,
That their frontal lobe lit up and oscillated.

You lean forward, your foot slips off the table
It suggests there's a heightened consciousness-
that visions of your family, the whole Heaven fable,
is your brain reassuring you through the process.

The process of death? *Of death.*
And I don't tell you this, and I know I should do:
When my heart stops I hope I'm lucid enough
That the remnant of my dying brain is you.

The Still Face Experiment

A mother sits opposite her baby,
maintaining eye contact as promised,
offering familiar noises, settling sounds,
thinking of other assurances she'd made
when she had signed the consent forms.

Her baby drools; the mother wipes it away.
The interview room is a controlled variable:
new sofa, new highchair, angled spotlights.
On the wall, blind behind her baby,
are two lights, a digital clock, a video camera.

When the red light signals, the timer begins,
and the lady looks away from her child,
like she's seen something in the new carpet,
or heard someone in the corridor outside,
and starts to count – let's say to twenty.

When she flicks her eyes back to her baby,
her stare is passive, empty to the object,
as though gazing through a fogged-up window.
Her baby doesn't understand the change,
the trick, or why her laugh echoes in the room.

Her baby waves, hides her face, tries to stand,
screeches, rocks the chair, bangs her hands
and legs in fits, thrusts her head as in seizure,
then stares at the new carpet, slumps still.
Spit drips down her open mouth and pools.

At the light's sudden signal, the mother lunges,
her eyes kind again. She draws her baby back
up into her arms, her smell, her voice, herself.
Her baby surfaces in resuscitated gasps of relief,
and clings to her mother. Tomorrow perhaps –

or in a few days – away from the camera, the clock,
the clipboards, imperceptible even were they there,
her baby will hold a little back from the mother
as if stepping away slightly from the edge of a hole,

after understanding the real
depth of the drop.

Wuthering Heights

You were exhilarated by the starkness,
marching the path past the parsonage in trim shoes
sliding over slick cobbles. Your goose-pimpled arms stretched
wider than the graveyard cedars,
Emily's tresses would have been billowing like this,
your tiny body a kite clapped against the draft.

The track soon shrank to wheel ruts,
then beetle brown earth, churned only by boot, by hoof.
Our steps slapped and cracked the saturated moor,
each path a gorge where rain giggled down
from the highbanking heather
and estuaried the morning's shower.

You allowed the wind to undress you,
let it press blue roses from your gown like petals,
cast them around the grey grasses, the wet white sounds,
until your colours could be found everywhere.
You saw the black grouse crash land on the gorse,
pointed out his wattle as the only red in his world,
then parsed the terminal buds by the waterfall –
the caramel yellow of a horse chestnut retreating.

The unclouded sky at the Heights was as blue as your chilled fingers
though a storm threatened afar like some distant sea
and a current was clinging to the air.
It drowned a man's voice nearby, choking the vowels
down his pharynx, *cold, in't it?*
and we trod the tumbledown timbers,
the toppled rooms, the withered ribcage
as though scouring a beached ship exposed by low tide.

So, the photographs you took from inside the wreck,
the leaning oak centered in the frame of the stone window,
don't show the nettles growing in the kickboard
at the blown in fireplace. They say nothing
of your damp feet, sheepshit covering them in frog spawn,
nor the fisherman's jumper you reluctantly accepted.
They tell not of your certainty, leaning on the wide windowsill,
Here. You are wildly smiling, *I think she stood here.*

Flotsam / Jetsam

i A dead boy on a beach

The boy's trousers have been taken down,
screwed low upon his pumps. A ragged t-shirt
has been tugged up over his nipples, over his head.
His stomach billows at the belly button,
it bloats as wet as a sail filled with waves,
like he has drunk seawater greedily.
Then the arch aches away

into gaunt hipbones, a gaping groin.
He is seven, eight perhaps; his underpants
are patterned with deflated footballs.
They've been sculpted back onto his dead frame,
mercifully. Though below this nappy,
his pinched knees are too brittle.
He is scarcely substantial enough
to have been born at all.

The wrinkled fist his hand has formed
is more fin than claw, he is barely there,
translucent, disappearing already,
laid out on the thinnest skin of tide.

ii L'Accalmie, Baie Saint-Paul

The bleached hull, sunk now into a white-washed shore,
moored at marram grass bollards
drifts on tides of sleep, currents of age.

Restharrow and sandwort knot it to the drydock,
only through cataract wheelhouse windows,
does a visiting sea silver near.

At dusk, while distant Montreal becomes campfire coals,
this beached boat trembles again its sinewy rigging,
checks thinned charts and maps a motionless voyage.

Soon, Cassiopiea dusts a rusty mast in diamond,
the Little Fox stalks nebula towards neglected nets,
and Cygnus hurries a shoal of stars onto the deck.

The sky, a saturate of swimming light,
The boat lulled into life by night.

iiii After the Wreck

Sometimes, when the last train brakes by the junction
it catches the track and sets off flares at the road crossing.
Lights search the sky then and I stir from my chair
by a cooled fire and go to hold the rattling window
to steady myself in the trembling room.

When the train pulls away, I stay there, stranded
in the same sinking darkness there was that night
the ship went down. The blind screams and muffled panic
of the desperate, the incoherent, the knowing, the gone.
All stripped and soundless in the sea.

Before the birds ring, I consort the pinkest horizon
and patrol the shore for survivors, mementos or something
that may anchor me to a fresh wreckage.
Among the chains that tie the boats to the beach
are burnt out campfires, balled-up bones of feathers and fish.

The chill seeps through my knees, I huddle into my coats
and hurry across the shore like a sandpiper,
picking over branches, broken pallets, crab lines
and wearied wood that has washed up here as I,
and will, each night, be buried again in these tides.

Turn, Turn, Turn

i summer: kingfisher

An eye peers out the prow of a moored boat,
Hyacinth floats past. A motor, distant, rasps
and, burnt brown below, the Mekong slunks slow

as sunset. Gathered like day old dragons
at our feet, five dogs gnaw a bitch's teats
and, bright as jacklight, above the red bank

on hanging branch, an azure kingfisher.
While we ponder its dive, our host arrives
with sugared coconut and dry ginger,

fills the dusty glasses with lime water,
peels cassava, rambutan, papaya
and a sampan stalks soft as he talks:

a neighbour fought with the US in the war,
teaching radiography in Saigon,
his seven sisters, his daughter abroad,

his white fedora, smoking like low tide,
conical hats, stray cats, the lit blue lamp
of the bird leaving the river's disguise.

ii autumn: hedgehog

Autumn is O shaped,
the narrow O of an echoing birdhouse,
the O below a naked flowerpot,
the O and broken O and O of rusty screw heads
in sodden patio chairs,
the O exploding from roman candles,
spinning spokes in Catherine wheels,
showy signatures by gloved sparklers,
it is the charred O left by the slow black bonfire.

Autumn is orbited
by the waxy O of the harvest moon,
the lost O when time forgets its face,
the yawning O of a tired nature retreating
past puddling paw prints
into brittle windy piles of leaves,
and furling up like the O of a hedgehog's sunken sleep,
the whorled up O of a mercury bulb-heart beating,
the annular O, autumn cheating winter.

iii spring: Blodwen

Whether you tripped and fell into the fissure
or were trodden down that crack by angry feet,
time failed to press you against its pages
and you slip out the soil after centuries -
a headless flower dropped from a dusty book.

Moss is a music scratched from your skeleton,
and silent spaces in your spine are beaten
and chorded into melody at the museum.
The score though - a crass, hunchbacked malady -
an arthritic, iron old lady embalmed in spotlight,

and pinioned to a gaunt board for display.
As a bog body, dragged from leathery torture to melt
like a guttering candle while cameras harrow,
your petals will flake, collapsing to bone-ash,
you will thin and hush and they will number your bones.

iv winter: the herd

The mist does not clear, instead the fog
from the fall thickens. In rich seams
of jewelled dark they adjust their lamps
and chisel the walls of the slide
for channels that heat the frozen hill,
a vein of winter fleeces in the snow.
A farmer is a giant treading the white sea,

bracing waves that break in whispers
beneath his feet. His crook plumbs
hopeful chimneys for his flock to find
but below him the pasture suffocates:
tracks are untrodden, trails maze,
lambs are born into their graves.

Romance is Dead

What's a heart anyway? A beating root
lethal as a fist, or a baby's skull
hung roughly on crossbones of ventricles,
some plumber's sketch, a plate from a car's log book.

Put your ear to a shell to hear it count time,
then tell me there's no romance to dripping taps,
siren sound, dogs barking in hot cars, trapped,
or the heavy steps of a steady climb.

Iron Age desire was forged in the brain,
Celts felt lust in their guts, the Greeks a quiver
from a love lodged in the spleen, the liver,
you give me your lips, your lungs and your womb,

keep your heart, leave me your windpipe instead,
so it can't ever be said romance is dead.

Gertrude's Truth

So close to have known
the wild flowers round her brow
buttercups, orchids, the coiled-nettle crown,
you trail her gown,

nearer to her mad tongue
and broken melody you stalk,
then, shy steps short of the brook,
you hear the chant haunting the wood unsing
in watery stillness.
There, you gather the news

over your shoulder
like a body, struggle with the strain,
the black stain it leaves 'till the guilt fits soon,
you deliver the death to her brother.

What is truth?
A report so young that words drip with dew,
Then puddle and grow so quickly green and stagnant
They could cloud memory and coronate
A kinder loss: Ophelia buoyed, jewelled,
Rests on the river's surface, barely deceased.
Truth can drown a suicide, can float a lie,
Can leave behind a mermaid on that tide.

Backstroke

From the jetsam of armbands and floats
Gathered in the shallow end
Like a slick, you heave yourself out of the pool

And hobble past the shivering girls with a runwalk
That makes the teacher splash her voice
And point to a fading wall, foggy with fading rules.

You dry your seaweedhair on my jumper,
Cling to my legs, as though they're lifebouys,
Count how quickly your wet footprints soak

And disappear into the floor. You tell me that,
If the water had no ledges or edges to fence it in,
You would have reached the sea with your backstroke

And carried on forever, swimming further, further,
Away from here. Away from me. So I stanch you
In a soft, white towel and suffocate your escape.

So tightly you stop growing. So tightly, you peep out
Over the robe, sealeyes, wetwhiskers, knowing now
That I was really always holding on to you. We change shape

Suddenly, but you treadwater, unwilling to be let go.
Your scapula undulates in the tide,
Big, brave breaths filled with teary burden.

And your arms, your back, boil with age.
Today I taught you how to grow away from me,
Yet here you are, being held, holding on.

The Hide

Yellow lights leans into the hide
like daffodils, warming the hands
of the trembling, dawn-eyed boy.
Peering at the pressed-open pages of his books,
it winks on the metal flask the father
filled and spilled earlier, beguiled by birds.

Before winter, by the gorse, the birds
next door's cat was too proud to hide
were quickly buried by the father
in a hole little bigger than his clumsy hands.
Then, like a story from a bedtime book,
he explained a little of death to the boy.

Once those words stopped flapping, the boy
perched by the window and breathed out birds
on the glass and coloured them in nature books.
He made a nest on his bed, hid the way birds hide.
As though feathers would burst from his hands,
he'd fan out his fingers and fly to his father.

The reedbed yawns a low, sad sound that the father
reassures is an old wind groaning, but when the boy
mimics the noise in his owl-cupped hands,
there is a commotion like a morning alarm and birds
burst from the blind grasses until the sight from the hide
is the same as the murmuration in the boy's books

and the starling sound is the quick-turning pages of books
and as the flock ferments and funnels, the father
says, *it feels like, right here, in this creaking hide,*
we're sat in the core of a greying storm. The boy
is hypnotised by the dark sky constelled in birds,
nature applauding itself, wings clapping like hands

and as the chorus relents, the pair link their hands
and the starlings drop as ash from burning books
back to their roosts. Soon the dawn sky is bare of birds.
Could you draw it, if you saw it again? says the father.
I could draw them forever, answers the boy
while the birds crackle like cinders around the hide.

After dusk, he hands his sketchbooks to his father
who cloaks his arm like a wing around the boy
as they leave. Yellow light drains from the hide.

Philanthropy

The family next door stopped throwing snowballs
When they saw me staring from the window.
They waved, but quickly left their deformed man
Half-built in the startlit square. It was dawn
When I finished him, when I got to sleep.

Most evenings, I water wallflowers
With praise, take them home, hold them 'till they're loved.
Then I tidy: iron the uniforms;
Fill breakfast bowls; squeeze some fresh juice. Last week,
I whispered stories to a dreaming boy.

When I cannot face work, I go to town,
Claim lost property at the train station,
And fill strangers pockets as they're passing.
Just mementos. Keepsakes - badges, books, coins.
I find lost kids in playgrounds for the toys

Or lay them on little graves. Little gifts.
In the summer, I grew sunflowers there
And put bedding plants on lonelier plots.
Sometimes the vicar helps me. Makes tea, talks
While I quietly fix stones, repoint paths

Until dusk passes and time takes me home.
On the common, the snowman's slipped and lies
In lumps like it's been thrown around a car.
I crash into my gate. Feel tight in the chest.
I must do something good before I'll rest.

Finding Moortown

In the bleaching sun
the car pants down summary lanes,
ticking like a wet mouthed hound,
leaping the rutted road, scorning brambles
when the grassy hackles sprang from the track.

At the corner by the Sticklepath turn,
it slows at a roadside stall, sniffing at your fortune
in the spiderwebbed tea cups for sale, recognising
your strokes in the unsigned watercolours,
the tea rings you patted onto paperbacks. A grey lady leans
on her trestle of living room junk, knowing
nothing of your name and growing tired
of the questions. The car nudges her for a nod,
a treat of anecdote, then sets off
after new scents, loping past proud buildings
hoping they will become Moortown.

Soon it sulks at the shuttered windows
of cluttered cottages and skulks
away from the rusty, growling gates of fenced in farms.
It chases its tail in a dusty, hopeless yard
then sits patiently, nosing up at a high hung sign
half hidden in hedgerow. The farm.

Barbed thistle nip at the car's belly,
horseflies strain at nostrils of open window
and claws click on the shale path,
announcing the engine's approach to the house
as a whine lit with want. Yellow triangles
bark back of guard dogs, fluorescent
coats in strangers' shapes wave us away
and a threshing machine door closes
in the windless morning like a trap.

The car halts and squats in the centre
of the farmstead, its ears pricked by a noise nearby:
a troubling ticktock, the flick of a mastiff's chain, the cocking
of shotgun, the faltering voltage of failure.

Against the paw of a tied up tractor,
a mistle thrush strikes at his snailshell in heavy,
percussive blows, charging your yard,
beating an anvil into submissive song.

Iago Prytherch is Standing in the Vestibule

Why then do you fly up to this hill's shoulder
While I quarry moles from the clouds
And tie their tails to trembling fencewire,
But to stare at a peasant's numb hands
And fret why God wields the forlorn fingers so?
Or draw my hangman's haul as lines and notes
To a vile music, dumb and remote?

In pulpit plumage, wings black as mass,
Your bone white head cruelly balances
Like a rook's beak and you become crow
Forcing famine down into the guts
Of wet notebooks until I approach
Waving the barrels of my weary arms
and you are dark feathers and air

Descending to haunted churches
To stalk meaning from the emptiness.
Sleepily I'll seek stars at soft fires
And you will lean long from your gloom
To poke again at my tired carcass
As though the furnace of my heart not yours
Requires meaning breathed into it.

What to do with his old clothes?

You carefully roll each babygrow from the dusty suitcase,
hold it in outstretched arms, weigh the memory of him inside it,
and fold it as gently as a paper bird. I unwind every sculpture again
so I too can inhale the months it wore him. Such quiet spaces,
smoky with his first dreams, warm from his growing world.

We carve out excuses that delay, then prolong the day,
He was wearing that on his first Christmas morning...
we could use those buttons from his cardigan, patchwork his pants.
I stack clothes into columns and we are made mute by the acute
understanding of what this operation means. We fold back the tears,

topple turrets into black bags, hold each other. There is a draft somewhere
and the room seems as poorly lit as it did when you were pregnant
and we painted the unfurnished house in wintery evenings after work.
I am as empty as the luggage at the foot of the loft ladder,
holding you, as barren as our busy lives will now become.

Downstairs, our boy is asleep, his body a Babel tower,
his loud breaths prising the baby gate ajar, his tiny flesh
growing up and against and through his pyjamas, his uniform,
his leather jacket, his woollen suit, his funeral coat. Tomorrow,
I will I put five bags in the car boot, one back in the attic.

Little Gods

We take our buckets to the pond
to gather up fronds of frogspawn -
running, as if those bleached eggs
might hatch while we delay,
or get gathered up like bladderwrack
in a neap tide of children's nets.
Perhaps, worst of all, those tiny planets fall
and crack open in their waxy dark,
down and away from our eyes.

If we don't see it happen
your voice raising like a thunderbolt,
then it doesn't count.
But, as the spume of frogspawn is glued,
far out of our reach, to a coot's nest,
we cup our shallow hands
to draw up dizzied tadpoles,
senseless in the trenches
between our draining fingers.

And because you can't see them happen
or hold them, outside in our dripping summer,
you miss the little flames grow
from their match heads,
and miss, behind the glass,
the water becoming gas green,
the pond weed losing its whiskers.
You are oblivious to them hanging there
in the murk, waiting to be watched

until you shape your fingers into a beak
and pluck them like coins from the bottom of a well,
study their knees and their straining lungs,
This one has eyes like hills.
This is as a grey as the rocks.
This one hasn't grown at all.
In your divinity you discover the dead,
dozens of small frogs, opaque as pearls.

We're just like Little Gods, aren't we Dad?
We empty the tank slowly onto the grass.

Gardening Leave

It was the first morning of a shirtless summer:
there were three wasps' nests hung up
in the shed roof like flower heads,
pallid peonies that itched with angry insects
when they were raked down upon cityscapes of paint pots;
sweet peas, relentlessly wrapping the ankles
of a tired trellis, were convinced to climb,
tendrils teased open and taught a vertical tongue;
bearded husks of lavender were pushed from a patio,
bulbs were pocketed in earth; the lawn was cropped
in close tram-lines and, while the motor idled
on the warmed tracks, three infant sunflowers,
repotted by tiny hands were staked to lollipop sticks.

The season was staggered by evening reaping:
watching her pick petals from powderwhites,
peacockblues; planting bunches in wine bottles.
Empty glasses, dinner plates, sitting late
until the sky reddened like blushing skin,
stopped once the dead linnet was discovered
brambled up at the fence and a thin, sloped grave
scratched in the clay swallowed the bird, the day,
the summer, the garden.

After the holidays, office clocks counted for longer
and the commute through the dusky rain
spread cars like rusty leaves across clogged carriageways.
Verges, urgent with wild flowers, were webbed by neglect.

And now there is no work. Only a wet-windowed leave
to tend a garden the winter can care for.
Just wasps patrolling the cracked shed window,
and ghosting reflections of birds.

The Wirral

So here is the Wirral, flat and moist and grey (Idris Davies)

But look left and each time your sight sails
to the breaking sea, steer it back to shale beaches,
over the close-mouthed coves,
the dunes, lighthouses, the sandstone spires,
towards those hills that carry the clouds.

These Welsh heights bluff the ramshackle piers
that lean and leer at the Atlantic, they collect
the creaking castles and drowned villages
in their cradles. They muffle the angry, Anglicised
come collect your benefits by the seaside,
and hide the second homes, the chapels for sale
along the nuclearglow, caravanslow coastline.

And while, to the right, Liverpool's hard stare
is softening now - its gap-toothed grinning docks
filled by shopping villages, tapas joints,
coffee franchises - it gleams still,
greedily as costume jewellery.
It is shackled to the same boasts of bright cathedrals
and brags of those boats that boil up the Mersey;
a drover dragging tourists to the city's ringing noise.

So turn left, towards that cloudier sky,
where the River Dee that rips Wirral from Wales
has retreated to the tides and the narrow estuary
is rolled out like a bolt of torn cloth.
Look across the sands,
your gaze stitching the landscape as a sampler,
embroidering paths home.

Yr Ysgwrn

The old and silenced harps are hung
On yonder willow trees again.   (in trans. From *War*, Hedd Wyn)

I've lost the word.
He is shrugging, winking,
thinking of which artifact he should summon
from a tablecloth chequered in the relics
that rested on Hedd Wyn's wartime farm.
Casting he nods with certainty. *Why*
is the handle of the cast iron kettle cold
when the base is burning?
The light limps into the parlour
and skulks those sat in a meagre silhouette.
It is too dark to read the spines of the books by the range,
too quiet to ask why ripped paper sags
and screens the beams. So, the old clock twitches
and the room leans nearer to the sheephaired storyteller
in his flatcap and to tales of his dead uncle,
the white crucifix, the black chair.

A hundred years ago in a shelter dug down
in some thudding field near Ypres, the man
must have measured how alike these trench trophies
were to the antlers above his mantelpiece;
known the barometer, grim behind mustard glass,
was as foggy as the one on the dresser,
that the uniformed boy cradling himself in sleep
rocked like the chair at the fire
and that the groaning, gathering din
was as inevitable as all his falling stalls, his failing crops.
Here too he could flake the bark off the beams
with his studded boots and see the rains bloat the wood,
could crook his forehead against a strut
like the one supporting his stable and know,
over the parapet, he would always be at war.

The handle is cold because the owner left it that way,
I think but do not say. The question simmers in silence.

Chrysalis

(Ty Mawr Wybrnant on the last day of the Easter break)

You raised the emptied acorn cup
like an offering, one palm steadying
the other, keeping it level to your nose;
so you can study it with giantwide eyes
as though a chrysalis cherishing life
and you might conjure its spell.

Your mother convinces you
to sow it in your jumperpocket,
so you can think tiredfeet over the doorframe
and measure your path across the flagged floor.
Drovers once gathered in this dark room,
all bullish in their noise, butting up to the hearth.

The warden strokes your head like a halo,
that tinybed consumed six sitting sleepers;
he shows why the windows were thinned of glass
and coaxes your mischief, chases you around the bibles,
plays hideandseek in William Morgan's tongues
and lets you slide down sheer steps as we leave.

When you roar a smiling goodbye,
he rewards you a chocolate egg –
undiscovered treasure from last Sunday's hunt –
you cup it in your hand,
this hollowshell, as you'd done the halfacorn.
when the house was still so big for you.

The Birthday Walk

The foreshore stirred in October sun
Though the harbour was stilled and flooded, the Grist slick,
   The reedbed listened and understood
       Jackdaws grieving
       In the hollow castle,
Crows oiling rusted wings, dogs chewing their wet yards.
I'd returned to find you on your birthday month
     But finding it hard,
     Turned instead,
   To tread the path around Sir John's Hill.

Oystercatchers chatter on the marsh,
And little gulls gather up in boathouse glances
   Of white against a grey-frowning sky.
       The track climbs
       Between half-clothed oaks,
My lungs lift, chest glowing like a robin's scarf,
So I undress half, fold the wings of a wintry coat
     Over my hooked arm
     And ascend
   Wearily up through the torn tree line

Where the path hangs loose as gossamer
Beside the breathing-blue broad window of the bay,
   And horseflies canter the dripping wood.
       Hidden down
       Low by tight-lipped boats
Church bells are counting and dog walkers loudly play.
Always, the hint of wind; always, the rumour of rain,
     Always sunlight sewn
     Up ahead
   Illuminating the autumn browns

And in shallow cloud by quarry steps
Forget-me-nots rest gentle heads on meadowsweet -
   While mine rests on colonies of words
       You consumed
       With your greedy tongue:
And repotted: sea-pink, Jack-by-the-hedge, windflower,
Or these marshes you mapped with your heart's hand.
   Kidwelli, Gower,
     All gone. Gone
   Back into the soil, the surf, the sand.

Yet the wood stays wet and the summit
Sings Carmarthen Bay as loud as the day you left,
   Bold breeze rocks the teeth of wire fences
       At the farm
       Where dairy cows crown
The horizon like cairns, sentinel to no one,
Cold as the matchstick tower on Ginst Point staring
       Out past emptiness.
       My gaze shakes
   Ghostly egrets out over the Tâf.

   And because you are not there, I sulk
Away from Pendine Sands, away from Rhossili
   Down mud, hooved trail, shade, gorse, down, backdown,
       Leaning lanes
       Through resting rooves, rooks,
Past gable ends where watery chimes are taut gallows,
Hedgerows are abandoned nests and weathervanes
       Are seized in the quiet
        sunbleached
   Nostalgia of your hunchbacked Laugharne.

   As yellowed nails on hoar-grey fingers
The council estate cresting Gosport Street lingers
   Like tarred memories of arteries you inhaled
       Lighting up
       October birthdays.
Or the wax drip left at the lip of mussel shells
By birds on drained bays when they scoop out their music.
       Wet routes are hollowed here;
        Cleared of you.
   Each year I feel your absence erupt.

Waking to find Wilfred Owen has left Craiglockhart

They are loudest this endless evening,
the dreams lit by war,
their moans again a bomb-blown earth heaving.

They stir to see the empty bed grieving
the man that left before.

And he, on his dark train, blind to hills, to hedge,
beehive, swallow dive,
to weeping wives lined at a platform edge,

will be dragged to Dover and thereby dredge
these men their lives.

His bedside – still candled – appears like distant flares
in gloomy gas
where the murky ward distorts hopeless prayers

from sleepless sounds: clock chimes; creaking stairs.
The night will not pass

'till cups shiver over saucers and spilled truths smoke
as the room awakes,
when the fact – they too must return – is spoken,

and all around will be bodies once broken,
wanting to rebreak.

Divining

The sun refused to relent this summer
until the soil had withered to a whisper
in the wide wildflower meadows
and the land revealed two tracks
it had kept secret for centuries.

For days, we counted jays down leaning lanes
climbed gates that had shrugged their hinges,
and prised apples from the orchard boughs,
where, one morning, you found the first furrow
and we trailed it to the woods of our world-edge.

You garnered seeds to mark a path back,
shrank when the crows clapped from the bank,
though soon you'd scouted the treeline for nests,
quarried toads from their burrows,
scratched our names in silver on the birches.

At the second avenue, you begged to explore alone
and left me at the limestone pavement to wait
while you tore the fissure through ash and yew
and returned with wild tales about waterfalls
and otter spoor and dropping rocks in a red pool

and you forged the bottomless day all the way home,
while the estuary shrank beyond the tight-lipped limes
and the windmills stilled. Before bedtime,
you drew the brook you'd divined and smelted
the warmest sunset in ore crayons.

We left without breakfast, tried to outpace
the empty roads as quick clouds filled the grey sky.
The wheelbarrow stands were stripped of lavender,
the egg boxes barren, the land prepared itself for the rain
that would silence our summer and close its paths again.

Two Paths Diverge in a Yellow Wood

i Edward Thomas

The road you thought you saw was chalk
Bone-white and buried, yet not by yellow light.
One destination to our wooded walk,
Never a diversion, nor fortuitous fork.
But one route, its end bent out of sight.

I enlisted earlier. Don't blush your derision
Swallow those words you would've hissed:
The chalk path is to be my blunder, my indecision;
these boots to etch their blunt incision
Like dulled shaving blades down a pale wrist.

This reply was typed with a ribbon that winds
One way, and in the terminal coil are trenches of ink,
So whether I write about landmines or lapwings
The print puddles. And, like mudded footprints
Towards war's emptiness, there the road must sink.

A line snaking straight down the centre of a slate,
Or earth, trodden and bruised, laced quick with lime,
I will follow this white path to France and state
That it was not two roads you saw diverge but time
Forcing open our friendship, forging my fate.

ii Robert Frost

The car aches along the highway,
slower than mourning. Such an empty
journey. A driver looks away
as she breathes by - wheezing, rheumy

to escape roads. I choose a turn,
another, then a track, a lane
and slow. I leave the engine idling
beneath willows and tramp a vein

through a field of sorrel and knapweed
(Elinor had called them *hardheads*)
towards birdsong at the glade's edge
where silver lines of birch are spread

like white headstones in golden pasture.
I rest there, incongruous, alone
and miss those I have shared quiet with.
Away, the car hums like our muted home.

Storm Arthur

The storm that threatened days ago,
reddening his morning moods
and throwing his temper in blasts of leaves,
now presses at his dreams as he sleeps,

bending them like the tops of trees.
It leans on the room, chokes it,
so his straining neck muscles
are as taut as telephone wires.

Sharp and dark in the cold spring night,
black words become trapped bats,
senseless and shapeless,
frenzied as they seek to escape.

He flinches at the fork of landing light
that shuffles him back into his starless set
and traps him there, in the growing heat
of his feverish midnight sheets.

By dawn, his blankets have slickened
and sweat gutters his skin.
Morning is puddled in the room,
and the place creaks as the sky shrugs

its debris - abandoned books,
sodden clothes, a yawning stillness.
The storm has passed. Somewhere,
on a far estate, dogs bark like thunder.

Dorothy Wordsworth's Grassmere Journal Open Beside your Hand

The wind was furious, the lake
as rough as corrugated sea.
Heartened, you urged it *no mistake*
to walk when skies turn mercury,
so we clung to routes the gale allowed
and sheltered below dripping boughs

then slate clouds hung on us like kites,
and all the world became the rain
that stung our brows from wettest heights
and spun us as two weathervanes
to Dove Cottage's disparate troves,
where I knelt at the parlour stove,

dried my cottons and wrote the day:
the honey-bee embroidery
of daffodils along the bay;
you, whiter than anemone,
charmed by celandine at the tarn;
skeletal deer blanched in the park.

While you read to rapt children, bounced
baby Thomas across wet knees,
then dressed, in warm, pressed clothes, and couched
that evening horizontally.
Your inward eye, ever glancing,
my journal, in your hands, dancing.

Pachyderm

I was the elephant in the room that summer
my skin thickening each day you did not call

from Brooklyn with news about the removals
job you'd spent the term shaping into an apple
with which you'd lead to me to and feed me

packing my lies snugly in the VISA forms
part-exing my rucksack for the roller trunk
you'd assured would be both safe and wardrobe
in flats furnished with seasonal labourers

obstinate to anything other than inbox alerts
or flights so cheap and fanciful I could afford
to dream I touched down and you were there
halfsmoking halflugging the front of a couch
off a van shrugging at me to gather up its arse end

I slept grey woke grey filled my childhood bed
threatened my keepers with sullen tusks
and carried myself back to university rehearsing
the silence I'd soon sit with in the centre of rooms
like a grand piano I'd stamped the ivories from
a mammoth suitcase obstructing the door

Voicemail

You are restless this evening, an old dog moping
from doorway to doorway, scavenging
sunbeams of memory to lie down against.
But these rooms are dark now, their outgrown photos
Turn away, tired of reminiscing.
So you skulk upstairs
                              and somehow, in pockets,
padded with tissues, hearing aid batteries
and subdued hands, your phone's linked to mine,
and your ghostly passage to bed recorded
as a muted message. Nights later you were dead.
This fragile voicemail, distorted
                              as distant radio,
becomes a monologue of your final days.
Silent, lonely, the faintest journey I've heard
until the recording cuts abruptly and leaves
just this wandering quiet we are both faced with.

Mr Larkin

He slapped me once, half-hearted, on my rear,
Then became furtive, stuttering, *Sorry,*
She asks for that sometimes, my Monica.
Gradually the thrusting limped, stung with worry

And stopped. *Shall we try again next Friday?*
After work – if you've nothing on that is.
And while I washed, he smoked, looking away.
This is my side of the bed. That's hers.

He took me the same places she showed him,
Day returns though – they'd share whole weeks away –
Castles, country houses, cafes on a whim,
All accompanied by her brash commentary.

We ate in restaurants they frequented,
Were always led to their smoking-room seats
Where, after ice-cream, until I relented
He'd rehearse my thighs with his shoe-less feet.

Back at the library, we seldom discussed
Anything other than the catalogue
Or shift patterns. But, yesterday, he fussed
Over my nails and filed a monologue

About his preferences of ladies' gloves.
It fitted us perfectly. Him being
Able to slip in and out of all loves,
Bar one – they wore one another like skin –

She was the only one he, really, took home.
If he'd put us others back on our shelves,
Not checked us out on permanent loan,
Would we have been happy? I ask myself.

Lambing Language

I couldn't fall. I felt her despair,
heard her pleading, but I couldn't fall.
Then there was warmth. Kneading passages
open, easing tubes. Warmth. Wet. The world convulsed and

I tumbled out heavily. Breathing ugly noises.
My fat tongue fooling each sound. But she shone
when I staggered around in her proud dewy words.

But I wouldn't give her quiet. Always I begged
for nourishment, slurred syllables as I suckled.
My eagerness tripped her, made her kick out
and she dragged me through bogs of plurals,
through webs of pronouns. Until we were weary,

hesitant. Though I found even bruises had names
and I felt bravery swell in my lungs.
She was in my ears always and I made her the middle
of every sentence I circled.

Others were swift to curse my clumsiness. I would trip
and I would hide in her, tasting the new noises
while she spat them in my defence.

In the mornings, I run: a bird on four legs, labelling
the world from behind the shallow walls. By evening,
I see shadows of how I may mutate: swollen
with syntax, fat with cliché, carelessly
shitting accidents until soiled language
greys my coat and I am too stubborn
to wipe it away.

When a farmer's accent stains my skin.
I will have become mutton in two tongues.

Perce Blackborow Stowed Away on the Endurance

By following the cat to the cradling shadows
the Captain had found me in the hull
rolling the ship's pet to sleep, folding its ears.

He kept his stowaways, fed us routine, purpose:
we were dripping echoes of his youth.

The ship's keel carved the water
for months and I filled a shivery diary
about the cold and the hounds and the quiet men.

I studied how the position of the sun
spoils photographs, scorns navigation. How it lights
thoughts of grey chapels in slate valleys.

Others hated leaving *Endurance* that night,
couldn't watch it snap and fold below packed ice
but I was soothed by our lonely landscape.

We fought nature's silences with stories, filled empty
spaces with football pitches and terraces of tents.
While men waited to be found, I explored

new whites that bordered the emptiness,
discovered how to stew a dog, feed it
to another. Savoured hanging heavy clothes

in the hopeful chill. Learnt how to hide
my limp from the surgeon's suspicions
by stepping forward first. Always.

Before the panic of flagwavers and cameras
at the quay, I shuffled numbly from the rescue boat,
Desperate to conceal how much I'd given to the snow.

But, in the stark room Shackleton led me to,
he made me sit and unwrap my boots.

I surrendered the raw black joints that day
as I submit to waves still; leaning on the balustrade
to hear a distant war stumble across the sea.

Casting Shadow

The sullen sky is subdued by the snow
and the morning brittleboned in the cold.
My grandfather's thermos smokes at the thawing lip
of the pit. The water is shivering.
I twist the willow halves of his rod tight
so the brass ferules fuse, wind in a borrowed reel,
and charge the circuit with a shock of green line.
My hands are gloved by frost and my fingers
hunt clumsily inside his tackle bag
for a tobacco tin filled with spinners.
I take out the purse of hooks and crude barbs,
a tablet-rack rattling hand-painted lures,
lead shot coagulated into boiled sweets;
floats, splintered, snapped – trodden as toy soldiers.
Set aside his two reels, both helmet green,
heavy as tank parts: one padlocked in rust;
the second suffocated with snared line.
The Sunday reedbed shuffles behind me,
an impatient congregation waiting
to be seated by winter. I cast cautiously,
weary of their heads – just as he taught me –
reel in his tales of jewels found in fishes' eyes.
In their mirrored flanks I see and understand
In each cast I make I shake his reflected hand.

Marrow

I wanted a collection of skulls while I was young. When
mammoth bones were being dredged from the North Sea
like turnips, I sought my own shelf of shapes:
a fox's secretive snarl and grainy bulb beak of a swan,
the polished fennel root of a rabbit. I expected to discover

them nostriling out of the back lawn like iceberged bones,
so I could summon them up with foraging fingers.

They would not need jaws hinging or teeth supergluing,
no pelt to peel or boil away; the soil would have sucked
all sinews, all pulse. No jackals could roam my room,
calling me from my sleep: the deer or wolf, the bear
would inhabit the cage of the brain in name alone.

I coveted beasts that age had thrown itself at in storms,
chiselling them from the cliff edges they'd been coffined.

There would be no space on the shelf for matchboxes
that rattled with shrew's snouts, thimbleheaded reptiles,
hurrying, scurrying insects whose colonies were smaller than crania.
I made my family understand I hunted only unicorns,
plundered divine animals that decayed

so many decades ago they had barely ever died.
Then today, I chased next door's cat from its cruelty

and found a swallow unzipped beneath a rosebush.
The fledging was frightening to my son who saw
his shallow mortality in the bird and begged me
to bury it deeper than any dinosaur,
beyond vertebra on a shelf of sand and silt.

'Pen marks on the pillowcase':
In Conversation with Glyn Edwards
John Lavin

John Lavin: The collection opens with 'The Land or Body Tide', which draws a parallel between the effect of solar and lunar gravity on the earth with the gestation of the human foetus. Simultaneously intensely personal and universal, it feels like a fitting entry point to a collection that is deeply concerned with parenthood, the natural world and our place in the universe. Indeed the poem feels like a distillation of your poetic aesthetic. Could you tell us something about not only what you are trying to achieve with this poem, but – broadly – with your poetry as a whole?

Glyn Edwards: I had fascinated over the invisible daily swelling of the earth's surface since encountering the concept of 'body tide' in a documentary. When I sought links between geological and physical forms there seemed many parallels with waves and surfaces and mass to explore. Though the ultrasound scans of my son were ultimately thrilling experiences, their memory is affected by slight sadness: as my wife and I left one appointment, the obstetrician asked us to hide the photograph until we had left the ward because, immediately outside her office doors, was a silent couple staring at a blank picture. I later discovered this appointment is known as a 'morphology scan'; the absence of the expected baby had, at that moment, hollowed the pair's capacity for language.

Visually, the poem presents this spine down the centre of the page. The number of lines in the poem represent the number of vertebrae in a newborn's spinal column and the number of poems in the collection. A poem about birth felt entirely appropriate for the first poem in the collection.

JL: Another key poem in the collection is 'Night Fishing', which feels like a metaphor for the creative process. The 'floating shadows' of the carp, 'too difficult to land', feel like poems remaining tantalisingly out of reach. Is this a correct reading? In terms of the creative process, do you feel that as you continue to write, even as your skill as a craftsperson increases, that the process becomes oddly less tangible?

GE: For a year or two, I'd wake abruptly with an idea I was desperate to record before I'd fall asleep again, so I would scramble in the dark for paper or a pen and scribble something without turning the light on. In the frenzy to record something lucid, I'd ignore the need to self-edit or the need to use the page correctly. In the morning, I'd often forgotten the incident and would wake to a dense crush of childish handwriting that I'd reassemble or elide completely. Sometimes there would be pen marks on the pillowcase or a glass spilt too. Many of the poems in this collection came from this process.

The 'carp' image is one of frustration. The poem that stares at you and knows that you are too eager to catch it. The poem that needs to be seized by surprise but has swollen into something so significant that to catch it unfairly would only ever result in disappointment. I tried to catch fish with a friend once in the pool behind his caravan and we had no idea how to do it. At the time we felt the huge, black carp were almost arrogant in how they lazed in the sun and we knew we could only catch them by throwing stones or clubbing them from the water. Perhaps, it was easier to speculate on fish the size of myth than to learn the hobby properly and to return at night.

JL: 'The thirty-three spinal vertebrae' mentioned in 'The Land or Body Tide' are reflected in the thirty-three poems of the collection, suggesting that the collection as a whole has a unity beyond the sum of its parts. I wonder, could we hear a little more about this theme?

GE: The vertebrae in 'The Land or Body Tide' is explicit and there is a reference to the spine in 'Marrow', the final poem, too; the same word is close to being the first and final words of the collection. There are poems that are fused into two or three or four parts the way that parts of the backbone amalgamate over a life. I intended the poems to be more about skeletons than the spine, insomuch as these poems are unified more by their awareness of mortality than the direct associations to the human frame. Many of the poems celebrate my young son, eulogise my wife, while others reflect on the lives of grandparents, or fictionalise traumatic moments in individual histories.

Having a maximum of thirty-three poems ensured there was a discipline to selecting the poems for the collection and I was often drawn to those ones with imagery of the body – organs, skin, skulls – so this quickly became a motif or theme in the book as a whole.

JL: You are a relatively new father and a number of these poems deal movingly with this theme. Parenthood is a difficult subject to get right without falling into the trap of cliché and sentimentality, yet in poems such as 'Storm Arthur' and *'What to do with his old clothes?'* you nimbly circumnavigate this obstacle. How did you go about approaching the subject?

GE: When my son was born, I felt a desire to chart every night time feeding in verse but these moments were too personal to be relatable; by adhering closely to the truth, they were too sharp with unqualified allusion, too doggerel in cliché. Poems like 'Little Gods' or 'Storm Arthur' used a memory to initiate a new narrative; there's enough distance from the faithful reality to be rooted in sentimentality yet malleable enough for a fresh fiction.

JL: 'Finding Moortown' deals with a visit to Ted Hughes' farmhouse and from a stylistic point of view is an unapologetic homage to Hughes. I'm presuming the poem recounts a real journey? Could you tell us a little about this and about the influence of Hughes on your writing?

GE: In some ways, I prefer Ted Hughes' poetry to poetry generally. *The Hawk in the Rain* was my first favourite collection and I learned from *Crow* how poetry can sustain a polyphony of voices that aren't necessarily the poet's. I read his letters recently with the same zeal as I read Dylan Thomas' in my twenties; I've bought and given away so many copies of *The Rattle Bag* to students as they head to university. He said, 'What excites my imagination is the war between vitality and death' and I feel that could be a mantra for all naturalistic writing.

Some years ago, we were on a family holiday in Hatherleigh in Devon and I was reading Hughes' *Moortown Diary* without knowing the farm where the poems had been written was minutes away. We drove in circles, losing the Sat Nav signal over and over, until we arrived at a farm that was industrial and empty and threatening. I sent this poem to Hughes' wife, Carol, and she wrote back to me, kindly, expressing reservations that we had found the wrong farm. The poem is a homage in a sense that, through its pastiche of

Hughes' imagery and tone, we 'found' Moortown, when, in actuality, we failed to. Although Hughes is now only one of many influences on my poetry, I am conscious that whatever I write, I may forever fail to find Moortown the way Hughes did.

JL: 'Marrow' opens with your childhood desire to collect skulls before drawing the collection to a close with your son begging you to bury a dead, 'unzipped' swallow deep in the ground, 'beyond vertebra on a shelf of sand and silt'. It feels like an appropriate way to summarise a collection that is always curious about and somewhat in awe of its surroundings; that is always, even in its darkest moments, in love with the joy of being alive, even as it is finding new reminders of the finite nature of our existence. And perhaps in that burial there is a sense too of finding out things through poetry that one would rather not find out about the world and perhaps about even oneself? Because, for me, *Vertebrae* also often feels like a book about your personal engagement with the creative process. Do you think this is true?

GE: It's a sadness of our time that frequently we only come close enough to study animals and birds when they are dead. It is a paradox that studying life in this way is believed morbid or unwholesome. Again, in this poem, I've changed many of circumstances: the bird was a blackcap and it wasn't unzipped – its neck hung to one side so I presume it had flown into a window. My son has been invigorated by his parents' celebration of stuffed animals and skulls, so he wanted to keep the bird as he had wanted to keep the bat and the shrew and the sparrowhawk. It is Arthur who collects rabbit bones and ram horns; it is his voice in this poem. And yet, he is my marrow, so the voice is mine too.

Today, we walked around a lake near Bethesda in North Wales called Cym Idwal. Charles Darwin had visited the valley at least twice and made discoveries on fossils and glaciers there. The wind was bracing enough to wipe our wet footprints quickly from the stone path. I considered telling my son how, compared to the loop of mountains, our lives are as brief as the prints on the rock, but I decided not to; he will find that out about the world in his own years. 'Marrow' is a poem about seeking discoveries of existence in order to justify existence.

JL: To continue with the metaphor of the buried swallow, if I may… do you feel as though writing poetry challenges your own perception of your internal censor? Do you find yourself writing about things that you are not especially comfortable thinking about, and would maybe not have thought about had you not been writing poetry? And are there times when you find poems going into areas that you're not willing to write about?

GE: The poem 'Voicemail' was difficult. I found an old message left on my phone from my grandmother, who'd called by accident and died weeks later. I heard her loneliness and her mumbling and felt her profound loss to the point where I called her back and left the phone in the empty house ring and ring and ring. She had given me a book of poetry by Rupert Brooke and this poem took the structure of a poem called 'Fragment' from his collected poems. His is a preliminary draft of a melancholy poem found in a notebook and published despite it being unfinished.

'Pachyderm' is an uncomfortable poem. The truth, that I was going to America one summer with a friend but was let down, became an investigation of sexual desire. The poem improved when the narrator's voice ceased being my own and became another – more desperate, more spiteful, more sexually curious – and the 'elephant in the room' immediately became 'the elephant in the poem'.

I wrote 'A Dead Boy on a Beach' in response to the infamous photograph in 2015 of a three year old washed up on a Turkish beach. While this image was listed in Time's 100 most influential images of all time, my poem was based on a photograph a week later of an older child. This image drew far less attention: interest in the Syrian Civil War event was declining; there was flesh and ribs and underwear present in the photo; there was a face looking back at a viewer; the body had been made gaunt by water. Though I considered it controversial, I tried to address the voyeurism that had been piqued by the national audience and social media's subsequent need for reminders of the conflict to disappear. It was the first time that I received negative feedback and I knew immediately that such poetry is essential to confront the silences that the national media construct.

JL: We've talked about Ted Hughes but I wonder if there are any other authors, or indeed artists of any discipline, that have acted as a particular source of inspiration to you?

GE: In his essay 'A Defence of Poetry', Shelley expounded on the 'rendering' of 'a thousand unapprehended combinations of thought' through imagery. He wrote, 'poetry lifts the veil from the hidden beauty of the world, and makes familiar objects be as if they were not familiar.' I have permanently on my bedside table Ocean Vuong's *Night Sky with Exit Wounds* and Andrew McMillan's *Playtime*; both poets have the rare capacity to make the regular events lucid. The influences of R. S. Thomas and Edward Thomas and Dylan Thomas have been profound at different stages of my life yet, more recently, I have enjoyed Hannah Sullivan's *Three Poems* and Robin Robertson's *The Long Take*. Ali Smith and Max Porter have been inspirational in the way their styles insist on experimenting; also in their ability to construct narrative from the environmental and sociological crises of our times.

A further source of inspiration has been the desire to compose a single body of poetic work. Initially, the creative need was to form solitary poems and to see them surviving in a wider domain – be that in magazines, anthologies or on the internet – and incrementally that objective became to comprise a series of poems in one book. *Vertebrae* is a construction that I am therefore very proud of; it is a rare thing to achieve one's aim. I will forever draw inspiration at contributing a collection to the wider body of literature.

Acknowledgements

Thank you to John Lavin for affirmation, for generosity, for time, for ceaseless support and for editorial guidance. Thank you to Jonathan Edwards for kind words here and always.

Thank you to Nic and Jane for reading everything first, and to Mum and Dad and Dave and Dot for reassurance. To Danny and Paris for adding music and film. To others who offered reading opportunities, or reading material, or patient advice. To those who simply listened.

Thank you to supportive head teachers, to encouraging colleagues and to proud students.
Thank you to Aida Birch and the Terry Hetherington Prize for Young Welsh Writers, to Alan Perry, to Rose Widlake. Thank you to tutors and postgraduates at MMU's Writing School, particularly to Nikolai, James, Jean, Danny and Rachel.

Several of the poems in this collection, first appeared in the following publications:
Cardiff Review, Dialogist, Eyeflash, The Fenland Reed, The Guardian, The Interpreter's House, The Lonely Crowd, The Lampeter Review, Nobel Gas Quarterly, Strix, The Use of English, Wales Arts Review.

'The Birthday Walk' was written during a residency at The Dylan Thomas Boathouse in Laugharne.

'Divining' was written as libretto for a composition by Ollie Lambert and performed by Joe Ashmore and the Marvolo Quartet.

An audio recording of 'Night Fishing' was featured in Dublin's first Poetry Jukebox as part of the 'Hungering and Migration' theme.

Find out more about The Lonely Press and our literary journal,
*The Lonely Crowd at **www.thelonelycrowd.org***